IDA

Searching For the Jazz Baby

FRANK PREM

LESLIE "SQUIZZY" TAYLOR

Publication Details

Title: *Ida: Searching for The Jazz Baby*
ISBN: 978-1-925963-84-7 (pbk)
ISBN: 978-1-925963-87-8 (ebk)

Published by Wild Arancini Press
Copyright © 2023 Frank Prem

Ida and Squizzy - A Summary - first published in *Meanwhile Murder: Short Stories of Detective Fiction C. CLancy, C. Radge Eds. (2022)*.

seeking (ida)

what is it
I seek . . .

it is
jazz

it is
the jazz baby

her name
is ida

Contents

About
Ida: Searching for The Jazz Baby

Ida: Searching for The Jazz Baby is a poetry collection that has its origins in the late 1970s when, as a young student psychiatric nurse, I took my place in the back wards of madness and senility that comprised a large portion of the Mayday Hills Psychiatric Hospital, once known as the Lunatic Asylum.

We had a number of elderly ladies resident in the wards, several of whom were named Ida.

Rumour suggested - without proof of any kind - that one of these ladies had been the once-notorious Ida Pender, gun-moll of Squizzy Taylor. Taylor was infamous as a gangster roaming the inner suburbs of Melbourne in the roaring '20s before being killed in a shootout with an arch rival in 1927.

Fast forward fifty years. I had just completed publication of a picture poetry collection involving images of Australian soldiers on The Western Front during World War I (*Sheep On The Somme, 2021*) and was looking around for another project from around that era - not another War book, but something . . .

Inevitably, I re-encountered Leslie (Squizzy) Taylor in newspaper records from just after the war, but without great interest on my part. He came across as having been a small-time thug and has been plentifully written about by others. Along with him, however, I met again the spectre of Ida Pender. And *she* was wonderful.

References to this young woman - a young girl initially - appeared in newspapers right across the country. Usually in connection with the activities of the gangster, but often in her own right and context, from the very earliest accounts of belonging to the local dancing class run by Miss Lillias.

Often portrayed as *accomplice* and *femme fatale*, she was at one stage described by Police on a Wanted Poster as being the possessor of '*shapely legs*'.

I found her story riveting and, seemingly, unexplored. So began my search for a woman who loved to dance, known as the *Jazz Baby*.

Before concluding this introduction, I have to express my appreciation for the NLA - the National Library of Australia (https://www.nla.gov.au/) for the wonderful online service that is Trove (https://trove.nla.gov.au/). It is simply invaluable.

FP
2022

Prelude: *My Ida*

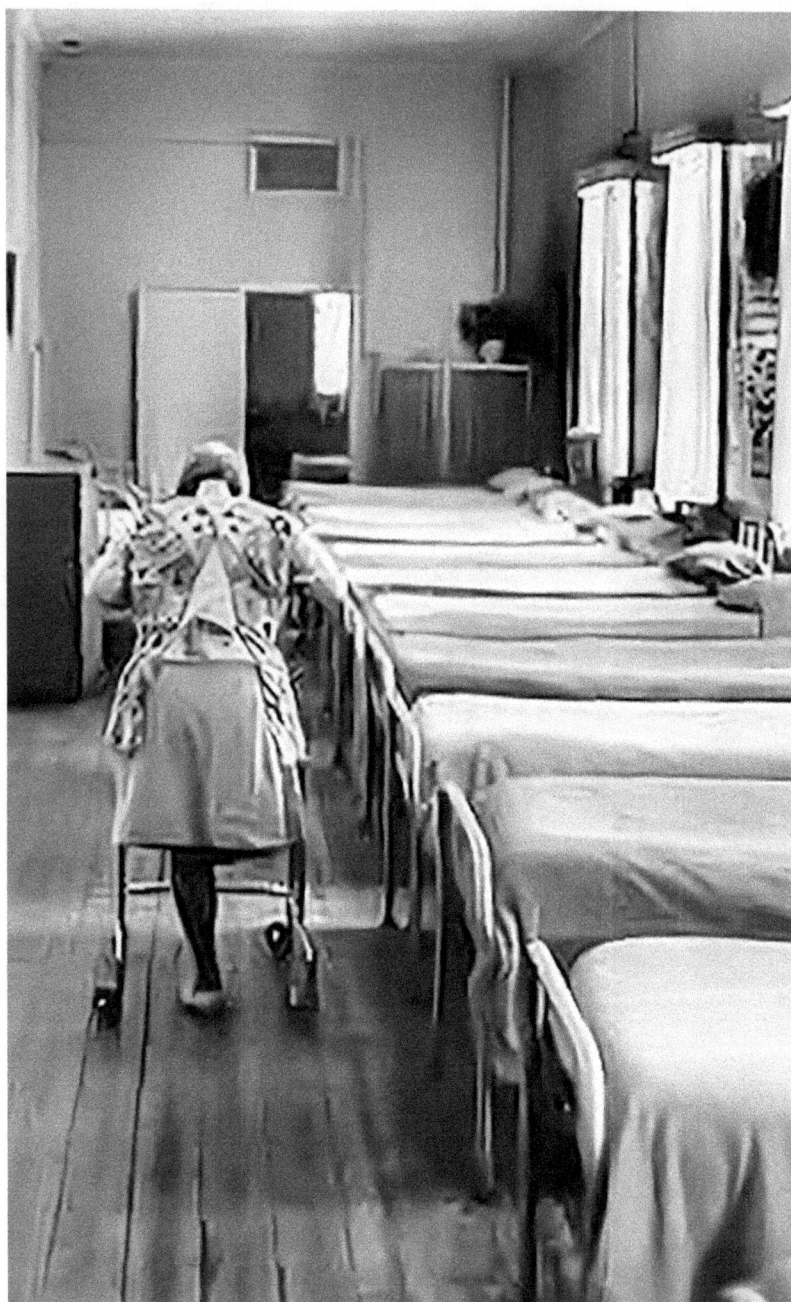

ida spider (I knew her when)

Evening Ghost Tours will take you through the deserted buildings, where your guide will share stories and myths of patients of likes of James Kelly, uncle of the notorious bush ranger Ned Kelly and Ida Pender the wife of gangster Squizzy Taylor.

Only Melbourne - Mayday Hills Asylum

oh . . .

yes

I remember ida

she was in the psychogeriatric ward
when I was a student nurse

back
in the late seventies

at least
everyone said –
all our amateur nurse-detectives –
that it was
her

she was thin
wasn't she

spindle legs

gaunt
bony arms
and face

deep dark eyes
that might have been hazel
once

I recall
she walked
incessantly

pacing

up and down
those long corridors
between the dormitory wings

never speaking
a word

then suddenly
she'd be there
right behind you
with her hands
shaped
into claws

just about
to strangle you

and her eyes –
then –
so nasty
looking . . .

gave me
the creeps

.

.

.

or
was it
the other one . . .

we had a couple
of ida's
in the old institution

one of them was blind
and deaf
and toothless

she used to squawk
constantly
like a parrot
unless they put a sheet
over her head
to get her to go
off
to sleep

no
that wasn't her

that one
was already
in her nineties

no
the other one
I'm thinking of
was a slender
reed

rosy cheeks
and bewilderment
was about all I recall
of her

anyway
they used to say
that she –
one of those three –
was her

our own ida-spider
was the gun-moll
of *squizzy taylor*
back
in the nineteen-twenties

until
he was shot dead

murdered

in the street

pow!

probably
it's just a story

the powerful woman

. . . Francesco Antonio (Frank Anthony) Labattaglia was the third husband of Squizzy's widow Ida Pender. They married in 1933, after Ida divorced her second husband George Lewin (aka Mickey Powell) in 1932, on the grounds of desertion.

Crime in Carlton: Last Drinks for Squizzy Taylor – 27/10/1927 Carlton Community History Group

I heard she
died
in seventy-one
but . . .

that can't be right
if she
is *my*
ida

and
I heard she married
three
or four times

my ida!

was she a woman
who stayed
near the inner city
and fitzroy
until she died

a woman who married
because a man
is a man
and
it can be
a dangerous life

or
was she already
mentally ailing
in nineteen
twenty-six

did she struggle
even then
with murderous demons
that stayed with her
all her days

and come
to her end
in the mayday hills
asylum. . .

in the psycho-geri ward
with her sheets
wet
every morning

and a line-up
each day before breakfast
for the shower
or perhaps
a dip
in the peninsula bath

there seems to be
a little bit
of mystery
about ida

my ida

I wonder
who
she really was
and who
she really is

and why
I
am letting her hold
so much
power

Jazz Baby

Miss Lillias Smith's Pupils Annual Display.

The Prahran Town Hall was crowded on Tuesday evening, December 16 when the pupils of Miss Lillias Smith gave their annual entertainment. They presented a most beautiful sight in their many varied and gorgeous costumes. Opening with Toyland, a beautiful scene, in which the children performed in a delightful manner, two little girls, Bonnie and Cissie Oldrieve, sang "The Land of Children's Dreams." They made a beautiful scene when, with the children, they floated off in a beautiful silver boat. The rest of the scene took place in Toyland, where a lovely little Fairy (Miss Edna Seggie), by the touch of her magic wand, brought all the toys to life. The Gollywogs caused much merriment when they sprang from their boxes. Misses Mellah Frizzell, Violet Bailey, Loris Wynch, and Violette Smith made very effective Gollywogs. The Dolls' Dance was very prettily danced, and the little girls looked charming in their frilly pale blue frocks and blue dolly bonnetts. In this were the Misses Doris Harper, Doris Reynolds, Dulcie Howard, Stella Hann, Nancy Bishop, Dolly Barclay, and Bonnie Lynch. Then came the Toy Soldiers, who marched in, just as you would expect toy soldiers to do. Those who took part in this were Misses Connie Barley, Iris Morris, Amy Prichard, Nancy Thomas, Maisie Stewart, and Jean King. Miss Marjorie Smith made a delightful French Doll in a beautiful lace frock with touches of pale pink and blue. She danced in a charming manner. As a Teddy Bear, little Lily Campbell did some remarkably fine acrobatic work. This beautiful scene was brought to a finish when the hour of midnight

with great charm. We think this one of Miss Smith's best scenes. The whole thing was truly beautiful, the finish and effect being all that could be desired. The programme then comprised dance and song numbers. Miss Amy Harris sang pleasingly "That Dear Old Home of Mine." A beautiful ballet of very tiny mites was "Sylvian Revels." Daintily dressed in white tulle, with silver wings and trimmings, Miss Kathleen Flitton was a smart little soloist. "La Orchid," by Miss Nancy Bishop, was a pretty little dance; her dress, representing the orchid, was quaintly made of violet and heliotrope shades. "Peaches in Georgia," sung by Miss Linda Stabb, with chorus of girls, was another very effective number. "Les Papillions" was danced by Misses Lila Jordan and Rita Bretherton, and these two little girls performed really difficult steps with ease and perfection. They wore beautiful pale blue ninon frocks, with silver tissue bands and huge butterfly wings. The "Skirt Dance, by Misses Dulcie Howard and Doris Reynolds, was cleverly danced. They wore sweet little shell pink tulle frocks, with quaint pink caps and blue streamers. A dramatic dance, "Jealousy and Death," by Miss Edna Seggie, was danced with fine expression. She wore a frock of black lace over yellow satin, and bead trimmings. Little Miss Sylvia Cook was another surprise in her song, "All Out of Step but Jim." The Ballet of Grasshoppers, Butterflies, Bees, Moths, and Firefly was prettily arranged. In this danced Misses Kitty Grey, Ina Grist, Ilene Preece, Connie Barley, Vera Moore, Gracie Brassington, Violet Pearson, and Elsie Richardson. Miss Mellah Frizzell, dressed to represent a beautiful white rose, then danced a pas seul with artistic grace and finish. The "Highland Fling" was cleverly danced by Miss Billie Golding, Miss

ida (turning)

It will be remembered that the pupils of Miss Smith were awarded the prize for the haunting set in the recent Prahran juvenile ball . . .

"Miss Lillias Smith's Pupils Annual Display." The Malvern Standard 03/01/1920

miss lillias
and her girls
perform
twice a year
in prahran town hall

how old –
I wonder –
is the youngest
girl performer

was it you
ida
at eight years old

did you begin
your dancing
with a lesson
back then

did your mother
perhaps
desire it of you

or
was it your own
true heart

you
took to the floor

the steps
and the twirls

and I think
perhaps
you could not stop
turning

to be (*jazz baby*)

Ida's dancing prowess derived in part from her lessons taken with Miss Lillias Smith of Prahran.

'Babe gets her name in the Paper', Croker Prize For Biography: Entry 1408. Author unknown

what did you learn
in miss lillias'
school

to spin . . .

pirouette . . .

to float as though
upon the air

and when did you first
learn
about *the palais* . . .

the palais de danse

and about escape
from your bedroom
in the night

to float across
a different air

jazz
a-ma-tazz

from
fourteen years old
in a dance class
to
sixteen
in the black night

oh
what a journey
for a girl

to be . . .

to become
the *jazz baby*

"SQUIZZY" TAYLOR---AS HE IS!

The King of Melbourne's Underworld.

MAN OF FASHION AND CRIMINALS' IDOL

An Arresting Pen Picture

(Exclusive to "THE MIRROR," by "ONE WHO KNOWS HIM.")

The most amazing figure among the criminal classes of Australia to-day is undoubtedly Leslie ("Squizzy") Taylor, whose many episodes in and out of the Melbourne courts have astonished the public for months past. The appended article is an intimate impression of Taylor by a person, now in Perth, who has met him and talked with him on many occasions.

Melbourne, with its gaiety, fashion and excitement, with its palatial hotels, its exclusive restaurants and its beautiful women, has been dubbed a city of joyous laughter. Yet it is also a city of whispers, sinister, significant whispers from its extensive underworld, that tell of debauchery and crime, of projected robbery, violence and even murder.

Down in the squalid, ill-lighted quarters, in the unpretentious tenements and gloomy bye-ways of South Melbourne and kindred retreats, crime and criminals are common topics of discussion. And one has but to move for a short period in this area to be struck by the fact that one name is mentioned more frequently than all others. Its denizens own one man as their chief, acknowledge him unhesitatingly as their superior. Mankind has always bowed down to intellect, and in Melbourne's underworld the inhabitants bow down to "Squizzy" Taylor, the master-mind of the city's criminal classes. If in seeking this remarkable man, one searches the lower quarters, looking

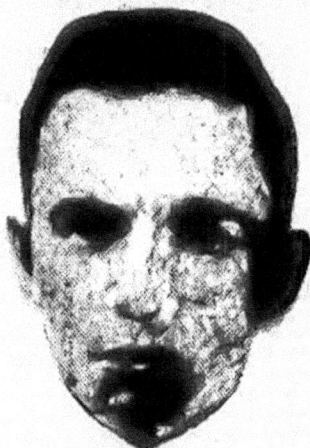

LESLIE "SQUIZZY" TAYLOR,
Leader of the Melbourne
Underworld.

for the master crook of the accented

the company (she keeps)

*The pair are "Squizzy" Taylor, and his paramour, Ida
Pender, who has been associated with him since she was
a mere child of sixteen*

"Squizzy" Taylor——As He Is! The Mirror, Perth 05/07/1924

is she
a *bad girl*

or
does she just choose
poor company . . .

> *a man*
> *might be a*
> *murderer*
> *but still be nice*
> *to me*
>
> *and*
> *if I love him . . .*
>
> *and*
> *I do love him . . .*
>
> *where else*
> *should I be*

is she a bad
bad girl

or is she
just . . .

just . . .

just keeping company
as best
she can

dance in the shadows (for leslie)

A man was in the drivers seat and in the back seat was a woman . . .

Ida Pender Arrested: The Age (Melbourne) 26/07/1922

babe

it's nineteen
twenty-two
you know

you're seventeen
and leslie
is *on a job*

come on . . .

be in it

wait
in the car –
motor running –
sit
beside the driver

there's money
and there's furs
and . . .

what won't you
do
for the thrill
of your man

babe

babe . . .

when the coppers
come

say
nothing

tell them
nothing
at all

leslie . . .

your leslie
will break you
free
from the cells

babe
in the shadow light
let me see you
dance

a gun he was (with a drooping eye)

He got the nickname because of a squint in one eye.

"Squizzy's" End: The Sun (Sydney) 28/10/1927

leslie was
a *spiv*
they said

sharp
and mean
and threatening

a very nasty
little man

handy with a gun –
the law could never
make a charge
stick –
but
he loved his girls . . .

all
of his girls –
with
a dangerous edge

and they loved
their
little man

ferociously

with loyalty

even though
he was *so* bad

even though
he dragged *them*
in

he was a gun
with a *squizzy* eye

and he loved
to dance

"Squizzy" Taylor's Reign Of Terror

Strutter, Schemer and Braggart

Ever lurking in the shadows, but known to be the planner of armed hold-ups, burglaries, blackmail coups and the terrorising of Crown witnesses, Leslie ("Squizzy") Taylor held despotic sway over a gang of dupes in Melbourne for 10 years from 1915 to 1925.

Describing this dictatorship of the underworld, Ex-Superintendent Frederick J. Piggott in this, the last of his series of reminiscences in crime detection strips away the glamor that surrounded the elusive "Squizzy," and describes several unfriendly encounters which he had with Taylor.

Crafty dark eyes under a rakish bowler hat, a stocky figure always wearing the best of suitings, a mouth ever curled into a sneer, and buttoned boots with tips of shoe grey cloth — such was "Squizzy" Taylor in the heyday of his crime dictatorship.

To us at the CID this immensely little fellow was a menace for years.

He was behind almost every major crime coup, his hand could be seen everywhere, but not himself. Taylor took meticulous care of his own person.

His dupes did the jobs and took the risks. He gave the orders, allotted the dividends, rounded up henchmen, terrorised witnesses, strutted here, there and everywhere, meddled in matters that did not concern him, and kept out of range of police revolvers.

Amazing Influence

Taylor was an underworld will-o'-the-wisp.

His influence over gunmen, burglars, pickpockets and safe-crackers was amazing. It amounted almost to hypnotism. Irresponsible youths just entering on a career of petty thieving elevated this dapper little braggart to the stature of a sort of demi-god. Underworld girls, too, were subject to the same mesmerism.

Wherever burglars, hold-up men, pickpockets and parasites on underworld women foregathered, the name of "The Turk"—Taylor's underworld title—was mentioned with awe.

He was the hero to an assorted crew of morons. But there was very little of the hero about "Squizzy" Taylor. He had plenty of low cunning, but when underworld factions fell out and bullets flew Taylor was always somewhere else. His arrogance led him into one such duel and it was his last.

Was Feeble-minded

I always believed Taylor had a mental kink. I do not suggest that he was insane, but my conviction is that he was feeble-minded. His mentality was immature. His brain was a mischievous, furtive, plotting brain. Sensational was feeble-minded. His mentality was immature. His brain was a mischievous, furtive, plotting brain. Sensational journalists did much to weave the spell and glamor that surrounded this little scamp.

Actually, he loved publicity. But he mostly threatened to get newspaper photographers who sought to take his picture. His was a mind that seemed to thrive on the turmoil associated with criminal records.

I tell myself to have much less to do with Taylor than certain other detectives, most of whom have now retired from the service. But Taylor hacked me heartily and the dislike was mutual.

He gave himself airs. Secure in the belief that he had a kind of bodyguard of gunmen and thugs always ready to do his bidding and secure in the belief that with money or menaces he could extricate himself from any trouble, he strutted round as a despot.

Should an attempted hold-up or other coup miscarry and a couple of his dupes fall into police hands, there was always a pliable agent at his command to threaten witnesses. Definite identifications of certain members of the gang often became vague and withdrawn by the time the case reached the Criminal Court or the General Sessions.

Witnesses were warned dramatically that they had better "break down" their positive identifications or the Colts automatic pistols would be turned on them. The intimation that this warning message had come direct from Mr. Taylor personally usually had the effect desired. Taylor, in this way, wrecked one or two cases I had built up against some of his henchmen.

His arrogance passed all bounds.

In 1924 I was searching for the man who shot and killed a bookmaker at Hampton. I walked into a Bourke Street hotel, now demolished, which then was used as a morning rendezvous by "Squizzy" and members of his gang. Taylor and a few of his close associates were in the bar.

"Hey, Piggott," he said to me, "you better call the dogs off in that pal. If you don't I will turn the Colts on

"That Little Bluffer"

"Why do you allow men of this class to hang around here all day?" I said to the manager of the hotel.

"I don't know them," he replied.

"Well, you will have to know them."

I said. They can come in and have a drink and get out. But they can't be allowed to use the place for hatching confidence stories and planning. If they do we will take action.

As I left the hotel on associate of Taylor's followed me into the Bourke Street.

"It won't do you any good to get the back of The Turk up, he said to me. He is a nasty man to fall out with."

"You get out of my way, too," I said to this man. "That little bluffer won't influence me in my job."

Some time later I was looking for certain stolen property. I decided to turn over a house at which Squizzy was staying in Carlton. We effected entry and Taylor stumbled round in his silk pyjamas swearing and fuming.

"What right have you to come in here, Piggott," he said. "I will get you yet."

"If you pull a gun on the sergeant, Taylor, a detective colleague of mine broke in, I will shoot you as dead as a rabbit."

The haul of Taylor was in the Glenhuntly hold-up which I investigated in June, 1924, and it was also in the demand for money with menaces made upon a well-known bookmaker a little earlier.

At Glenhuntly it was a case that was playing upon in a huge amount of lovers and villainy was in its element. A ring on the door bell was answered and four men strode in. Three of them wore black masks and one of them a white mask. All of them wore revolvers and they forced the man who opened the door to precede them up the stairs. Once man remained on guard outside, and the others walked into the room where the card players were.

"Hands up," they ordered. They took

besotted (said detective piggott)

*Irresponsible youths just entering on a career of petty
thieving elevated this dapper little braggart to the stature
of a sort of demi-god. Underworld girls, too, were subject
to the same mesmerism."*

"Ex-Superintendent F. J. Piggott describes" The Herald,
Melbourne 06/02/1935

detective piggott
said

> *they make him out*
> *some sort*
> *of demi-god*
>
> *a crafty eye*
> *and*
> *a curling sneer*
>
> *he wears the best*
> *of suits*
> *with*
> *a velvet collar*
> *and*
> *black bowler hat*
>
> *he's little more*
> *than*
> *a snazzy little*
> *villain . . .*
>
> *and a murderer*
> *they idolize*
>
> *and furthermore . . .*

said detective piggott

the girls –

sad
underworld besotted
creatures –

all of them
seem quite ready
to do
more

preserve her purity, yes (but not with us)

. . . like the time a Catholic mother discovered her daughter was sleeping with Taylor the gangster, so she promptly packed the girl off to a convent . . .

Batman's Melbourne, The Bulletin, Sydney 10/05/1969

*it is a matter
of regret*

think of the convent . . .

the nuns . . .

the other girls

*we are sorry
but
it cannot be*

*for –
as much
as it is a part
of our convent mission
to save
a girl from bad
company*

*loose ways and foolish
carnal
infatuations –*

*the threat
is real*

*and a fire
is real and . . .*

mr taylor
and his threats
are very much
too real
to ignore

so your girl
your wayward
daughter
has to return home

there is no place
for her
with us

and you –
her mother –
must find
some other way
to keep her
pure

IDA PENDER ARRESTED

"THE WOMAN IN THE RED CLOAK."

DETECTIVE'S LUCKY MEETING.

An interesting arrest was made in Melbourne on Tuesday. The accused person is Ida Pender—or, as she is more generally known, "Babe" Pender, whose name had been associated with that of "Squizzy" Taylor during the past few months.

In the early morning of March 7 a constable and a night watchman were patrolling together in Glen Huntly-road, Elsternwick, near its junction with Orrong-road. As they approached the cross road they saw a motor car, with lights extinguished, standing about 20 yards up Orrong-road. A man was in the driver's seat, and in the back seat was a woman wearing a brilliant scarlet opera cloak. The policeman and his companion were then attracted by a noise to a row of lock-up shops in Glen Huntly-road. They called out, and two women and a man, all carrying parcels, ran out. In their hurry they dropped their burdens in the road and dashed for the car, which had started to move. The three boarded the vehicle as it gathered speed, and it drove away, although the constable fired several shots. The following day Percy Speakman, motor driver, was arrested and charged with breaking into the shop of Rita Moore, and stealing property valued at £321. Later Albert McDonald and a man named Johansen were arrested on a similar charge. Some days after the burglary Ida Pender was identified by the watchman as the "woman in the red cloak." She made a statement to the police and was detained by the police at a country town as a witness. However, the constable who was put on to guard her left her one day while he went for a shave. When he returned she was gone. From then until Tuesday her whereabouts were unknown.

In the meantime Speakman was tried. The first jury disagreed, and the second found him not guilty, and he was discharged. Then, for want of sufficient

the window, and when Madin said "Hullo, Ida," she immediately walked over to the police. Madin told her there was a warrant out for her arrest in connection with the Elsternwick robbery, and she accompanied them to Russell-street. She was very self-possessed, and referred in an amused fashion to the way the police had been searching for her and Mr. Taylor. "The petrol you used must have cost a lot," she said, smiling.

At the city watchhouse she was charged with breaking into Mrs. Moore's shop. She was almost immediately released on bail, a surety entering into a bond of £100 for her appearance at the City Court on Friday.

a shimmer shape (in a scarlet cape)

. . . and in the back seat was a woman wearing a brilliant scarlet opera -cloak.

Pender Arrested The Age, Melbourne 26/07/1922

was that you
ida . . .

they said you wore
a scarlet cloak

brilliant scarlet

that you were
waiting

while *squizzy* stole
the stoles

and the furs

and dresses

they held you
in a lock-up
but . . .

perhaps
you played
your charms . . .

. . . in such a way . . .

in
such
a way . . .

you disappeared
as though you'd never been

a curl of smoke

a shimmered shape

left
drifting on the air
before
a startled
young constable

as it transpires (I believe)

*. . . had managed recently to get into Pentridge Prison
as a member of a concert entertainment party, and had
spoken to her husband, Leslie ("Squizzy") Taylor . . .*

*"To See "Squizzy." The Daily Standard, Brisbane
26/09/1924*

leslie
has gone away
for awhile

they've locked him up
in jail
again

taken him away
and
they don't like
young girls
like ida
coming round

no
they don't want
a young thing
disturbing the peaceful life
of pentridge

but faith
has a way
of uniting lovers
even with stone walls
in the way

while belief
is a love song
sung through
the cell bars

and *I* believe
and *I*
have faith
that
ida will find him
and
see him

though the walls
of the pen
loom
so high

with faith
and
with song to inspire

love will triumph
and a visit
will
transpire

ST. KILDA DRAMA

IDA PENDER'S STORY

Loves the Sea

Who is Ida Muriel Pender, the young mystery woman, whose presence at 443 arkly street. St. Kilda, has linked her ame with the dramatic incident of Angus Murray's recapture in Melbourne?

Known to her associates as "Babe," his woman with the big grey eyes talked to a representative of the Melbourne "Herald" yesterday, about herself. She is 18 years old, with a head curly brown bobbed hair.

"My earliest recollection," she said, s of the sea. When I was about five spent most of the summer days in the ater. I was born at Brighton, and so hen have I always been on swimming hat I have never lived far from the sea. "My father is dead. I cannot remember him, but it was always my mother ho encouraged me in outdoor games nd other healthy exercise.

DISLIKED LEARNING

"My first lessons were at a Brighton ndergarten. I did not bother much bout learning, for I was mad about the a and regarded swimming as the most mportant thing. After that I went to hool at Elsternwick and gained both e junior and senior certificates for vimming and one for proficiency in st-aid. Those were happy days.

"I went to Sorell's to learn the milli ry business. The experience gained iere has been useful to me. It has lped me to judge instantaneously if a it will suit me or not. Leslie doesn't ink it right for a young girl to be out illivanting too much, but whenever he kes me I always choose a dancing hall the pictures. I am not particularly en on the theatre, and don't think the cecourse the place for any women. I ve been there twice only, on big race ys.

"In the evening when we are not out ere is always the gramophone. I'll ow it to you."

show it to you."

ST. KILDA HOUSE.

She led the way to the drawing roc with its Jacobean furniture and Wil pile carpet. The walls were decora principally with photographs of frien but there were five of Leslie Taylor. "How did you come to be known 'Babe?'"

"That was my mother's doing." replied. "She never called me anythi lse. Everybody has followed suit. uppose they think it suits me. . All the same I am really grown up. you could only wait you would see wl an excellent lunch I will be prepari

as important (as an excellent lunch)

*I did not bother much about learning, for I was mad
about the sea and regarded swimming as the most
important thing*

"St Kilda Drama" News, Adelaide 13/10/1923

*the most
important
thing*

how to judge
among the *this*
and the *that*
is
a complicated
task

especially
when you are
young

I was always
my mama's *babe*

always everybody's
babe

but
more grown up
than anyone
can tell

than anyone believes

watch . . .

watch me prepare
an excellent lunch
simply
an *excellent* lunch

just as
a woman must do

leslie doesn't like
me
going out
much
for he thinks me too young
but . . .

when I do
it is the dance halls

the *palais*
or
the *green room*
or . . .

I also enjoy
skating

did you enjoy
the lunch
I made
for you

in emergency colours (I'll come back for you)

A heroic jockey (Taylor) saves his girlfriend (Pender), the daughter of a horse trainer, from a criminal gang determined to stop him from riding the race favourite to win in the Eclipse Steeplechase.

"A Prohibited Picture." The Sydney Morning Herald 03/11/1922

come on
ida
let's ride the track

the flats
or jumps
or . . .

I don't care

being famous
is fantastic
and
being bad
is
being free

we can make
a movie
starring
the two of us

I
will be the jockey
and
the hero

but never fear

no

never fear

I will come –
in the final reel –
to save you

you know
I'll *always* come back
for you

ABOVE ALL

The Sun

FOR AUSTRALIA

NEWS ~ PICTORIAL

IONE: 11633.

MELBOURNE: FRIDAY, SEPTEMBER 22, 1922

(Registered at Melbourne, for sion by post as

LONG SEARCH ENDS --- "SQUIZZY" SURRENDERS

meet leslie (we're in the papers)

Long Search Ends . . . Squizzy Surrenders

*Squizzy Taylor surrenders to police, The Sun, Melbourne
22/09/1922*

hello

meet leslie

it is true
he is small-ish man
of only five
feet and
two inches

so what

and
it is true –
they say –
that he is bad
in
all kinds of ways

so what

so what
and why
should I care

he dresses well
and
buys me things
and . . .

and
he takes me
dancing

sometimes
it can be
a dangerous life
but
the coppers
don't know
(anything)

and the coppers
can't touch
(anything)

we're in
the papers
almost
every day

people know him . . .

and they
know *me*

he calls me
baby baby

that's
his name
for me

meet
leslie

ELSTERNWICK.—6.3.22.—Pender, Ida, is charged, on warrant, with feloniously breaking and entering the shop of Rita Moore, 183 Glenhuntly-road, Elsternwick, with intent to steal, and did steal a georgette frock; 5 sponge cloth frocks; a number of blouses; and other articles, value £221, at Elsternwick. Description:—16½ years, looks older, 5 ft. 4 in., medium build, active appearance, brown hair (bobbed), shapely legs, dressed in a reddish-brown coat and skirt with suede lapels, black blocked felt hat, long veil; fashionably dressed. Fond of jazzing and skating. Is an associate of "Squizzy" Taylor.—O.2913. 29th March, 1922.

I'm ida (who are you)

. . . is charged on warrant

Tenille Hands, "Squizzy Taylor, the reel-life gang-star",
National Film and Sound Archive

oh
I'm just a girl
from elsternwick

I was born
near there
in brighton
so
I haven't moved around
very much

I learned to dance
with *miss lillias*
and
she would have us all
perform –
in public –
to a dance list
that we practiced

some of the girls
sang
but I was always
more interested
in moving around
and feeling
like I was free

when I was a kid –
(I'm eighteen
now) –

I used to climb
out of my bedroom
window

in the nighttime

and I'd find my way
to st kilda . . .

to *the palais*
or *the green room*

I was too
young
really . . .

I know that

but
oh that music
just needed
for me to dance

I still love
to dance

jazz

they say that I'm
a *jazzer*

I suppose
I must be
because
I love it so

that's
where I met
leslie

he was
so
good looking
and well dressed

he loved
the way I moved

he makes me happy

anyway
that's all I have
to say
about me

I don't want to speak
about my picture
in the paper

that was just
a misunderstanding

I'm ida
that's all

what's *your* name

there is always the gramophone (I'll show you)

The experience gained there has been useful to me. It has helped me to judge instantaneously if a hat will suit me or not

"St Kilda Drama" News, Adelaide 13/10/1923

I can't really
say
how it happened

we just met
and suited each other
somehow

it was
at the palais
when I was dancing
and
I still love to dance
whenever leslie
will take me

if I get to choose
it will be
a dance hall

or
the pictures

in the evening
if we don't go out
there is always
the gramophone

here
I'll show it
to you

they wear out their tires (then let me go)

. . . while she was looking in Ball and Welch's window

"Mystery Heroine" The Herald, Melbourne 11/10/1923

it is strange
to read about
myself. . .
in the newspapers

I try not
to look for any
of their
attentions

but leslie
is a little bit
famous

and I suppose they think
that writing
about me
is a way
of writing about him
too

they arrested me
once
when I was just looking
into a shop window

at the dresses
and clothes

that was detective
madin

he
had already worn out
a set of tires
on his police car
looking for leslie
before he settled
on me

he had to let me go
though

they always
have to let me
go

"Squizzy" Taylor Divorced

Wife Abandons Conjugal Field

In Favour of Ida Pender

Theodore Joseph Lester Taylor, known generally over East as Leslie Taylor, and colloquially as "Squizzy," 'has passed another milestone in his hectic career of 36 summers.

His wife, described by her counsel as a respectable young woman has divorced him.

She has left the joys of the conjugal field entirely to Ida Pender.

Nobody was able to give the court any light about Taylor's means or the fountain spring of his fabulous wealth. His wife said he had always plenty of money.

She wanted more than the £3 a week that Taylor had been allowing her for herself and their child. Alimony, however, was reserved in the absence of specific information about Taylor's income.

Taylor's wife was Irene Lorna Taylor, 21 years of age, of McCracken-street, Kensington, and she sought divorce in the Melbourne Divorce Court from Theodore Joseph Lester Taylor (known generally as Leslie Taylor, or otherwise as "Squizzy" Taylor), 36, on the ground of misconduct with Ida Pender. There was no appearance of the husband, and after hearing the evidence, Mr. Justice McArthur granted a decree nisi.

COUNSEL'S STATEMENT.

The case created a good deal of attention, and the court was filled with spectators. Mr. T. Power (instructed by Mr. E. J. V. Nigan)appeared for the petitioner, a fair, well-proportioned young woman, nicely dressed in a light brown frock, and having on a large hat which hid most of her face.

In opening the case, counsel said that he would be able to show that the respondent, who was supposed to be a bookmaker's clerk, got into trouble with the police, left his home, and had for some time lived as man and wife with Ida Pender, a young woman to whom he had apparently become attached.

Wife (to disappointed horse-owner): "Mrs. Hampson was telling me about a lucky horseman who came over from Melbourne last Easter. He brought over eight horses. Not one of them got a place in a race, and yet he made quite a lot of money out of them".

Hubby (gruffly): "I suppose he had the bookmaker laying them".

Wife: "No, dear; he had a merry-go-round".

"Petitioner," counsel added. "also claims alimony. He has been allowing her £3 a week for the support of herself and child. She claims that £4 or £5 would better fit the circumstances, but as to what Taylor's exact financial means are I have no information."

THE MARRIAGE.

Petitioner, in her evidence and affidavit, stated that she was married to respondent on May 19, 1920, at Fitzroy, according to the rites of the Congregational Church. There is one child, a female, Lesley Taylor, born at St. Kilda on October 6, 1922. She was now in witness' custody. Another female child, June Taylor, was born on June 5, and lived but seven months. At the time of marriage respondent was a horse trainer.

Mr. Power: After marriage you and your husband resided together, where?

Mrs. Taylor: We went to Epsom-road, Caulfield, for a period of 18 months, and resided in a boarding-house. He paid for our board. Then he bought a house, paying about £1,400 for it, in Station-street, Caulfield, and we resided there for five months. I left and went to Addison-street, St. Kilda, and boarded there. My husband used to visit me from time to time, and it was there that our present child was born. About this time he was arrested.

His Honor: Was he in gaol?—No.

After his arrest he kept away for about 12 months.

He absconded from his bail?—Yes.

tell them nothing (but a lie)

He said that what I had been told concerning Ida Pender
was all lies.

""Squizzy" Taylor Divorced" Truth, Perth 08/03/1924

it's so easy
to tell
a lie

leslie
does it

that old wife
of his –

she says
she is twenty-one
but
I think
she might be
older –

she lies
too

they all
tell lies

I try not to

there is no need
to tell lies
when
you can dance

I love jazz
you know

as for the police . . .

oh well

I try not to tell them
anything

jobbing dancing (moving)

. . . it was this girl who led Ida's footsteps into the underworld where "Squizzy" was king

"Ida Pender's Hard Fight To Live Down Unhappy Past"
Smith's Weekly, Sydney 09/06/1928

school
was never any good
for me

I had to leave

so –
when I was still
fifteen –
I left

I worked
then
at mrs palotta's
millinery shop
in the centreway

that was
my first job
and
I was learning things
that were important

hats
are important

and mrs palotta
and the staff . . .

they were
wonderful

I thought they were
the most important people
in the world

my friend there –
the senior milliner –

she took me
one day
to the palais

you know
the *palais de danse*

and I was hooked

I learned a lot
with miss lillias but
jazz . . .

jazz was something
more

something free

and I met people
there

so many interesting people

it wasn't long
before I was jumping out
of my bedroom window
to meet up
with my friend
and go
dancing

she introduced me
to leslie
at the palais

he liked the way
I moved

confused (yet right)

When he brought her back they lived openly together.
Leslie's wife divorced him, and Patricia was born in
"wedlock".

"Ida Pender's Hard Fight To Live Down Unhappy Past"
Smith's Weekly, Sydney 09/06/1928

patricia

it's a lovely name
for a girl

little pat

and her grandma
loves her
though leslie thinks
maybe
she loves her
too much

they don't get on
so well
my mother
and leslie

but he dotes . . .
just dotes
on *little pat*

sometimes
when I look around
and don't really know
who I am
or what
or
how I came to be
here

I see *little pat*
and think
I must have done
something
right . . .

we
must have done
something
right

other times
I just feel
confused

long ago (right now)

Ida Pender was employed, as a waitress at a big club in Melbourne. Like hundreds of others, married, women and widows, who-find it impolite to work in cafes and restaurants under their own names, she assumed the name of "Miss Henderson."

"Ida Pender's Hard Fight To Live Down Unhappy Past"
Smith's Weekly, Sydney 09/06/1928

after leslie died
well
it was a terrible time

we had seven years
together

seven years
and a daughter

then
he was gone

of course
my mother
took me back
and helped
to look after patsy

and I went out
looking
for work

leslie would shower me
with money
when he had some
but
when he died . . .

there was nothing

he didn't own
a thing

and we needed money

I enjoyed
waitressing
but
I couldn't tell them
who
I was

there were too many
men –
from those
other days –
would have liked to have a piece
of something –
someone –
that leslie had owned
or been with

bad men
really

eventually
I was found out
and then
I couldn't work
at all

it's so
unfair

it seems as if
all that is left
for a widow like me
is to find a man
again

to support me . . .

and little patsy

well
well
if I need to
I can

it all seems
so long ago
already

Postscript

and so (good night)

and so . . .

you are gone

never *my* ida
at all

did you sail
into a sunset

dancing your jazz
holding patsy
by the hand

across the floors
of your *palais*
de life

I hope
that you did

and I want
that you did

farewell
jazz baby

good night

Classic and Character Dancing.

By Pupils of Miss Lillias Smith.

A juvenile entertainment was given in the Prahran City Hall on Wednesday evening in classic and character dancing, song scenas, &., by pupils of Miss Lillias Smith. Similar entertainments are provided annually by Miss Smith, and are always looked forward to with pleasure. That on Wednesday evening, from an artistic and classical standpoint, was quite up to the usual high standard, if not better. Miss Lillias Smith is a recognised expert teacher, and Wednesday evening's splendid programme reflected the greatest credit upon her. There was a large audience present, and they were delighted with the whole of the programme, a lengthy one, from start to finish. The majority of the younger artists acquitted themselves real well, and those older in years gave displays in pas seuls, classical dances, ballets, etc., that were extremely fine. There were exhibitions in general deportment that were artistic and naturally graceful. We append the programme of items as printed. It would be really invidious to single out any of the artists for special praise. There were many charming costumes worn by pretty girls, and as all contributed so well towards the lengthy programme, to particularise would be superfluous. There was some surprisingly good toe dancing, and this the audience heartily applauded. Miss Lillias Smith herself favored with an item, and, needless to say, achieved a decidedly artistic success, her effort calling forth loud applause. For all round efficiency in dancing, Miss Smith's numerous pupils are in the forefront in Prahran.

Di Gilio's band provided the music, Miss George officiating as pianiste. The enchantment of the dances was made the more effective by the aid of Gunn's limelight effects.

At the conclusion of the entertainment the children engaged in a short programme of ballroom dancing, and they, like the audience, enjoyed themselves thoroughly.

The items as programmed for Wednesday evening were as follows:

1. **Irish Scene.** Misses Ilma James, Maisie Stewart, Olive Barnes, Stella Sinnott, Paula Wells, Vera Moore, Irma Cook, Violet McDonald, Nancy Caplin, Gracie Arnold, Ida Pender, Leona Wynch, Stella Hann, Norma Skewes, Dulcie Howard, Doris Reynolds, Jimmie Golding, Thelma Scott, Jean Stone, Frances Molyneux, Kitty Grey, Edna Seggie, and Marjorie Smith, and Misses Hogan and Robb.
2. **Danse De La Nymphs.** Misses Verna McCartney, Linda Stabb, Violette Smith, and Violet Bailey.
3. **Dance—"Folly."** Misses Billie and Jimmie Golding.
4. **Kittens' Parade.** Misses Norma Skewes, Frances Williamson, Sylvia Cook, and Kevan Graham.

ida and squizzy – a summary

"For years after his death she was seen dancing there regularly; in the early 1930s locals called her the "Angel of Death"

Seaside saga - The Age, Melbourne, July 16, 2004

Ballet - "Irish Scene"

twenty four girls
all
a-giggle

miss lillias smith's pupils
in performance

was it taffeta
and tulle
and rustling skirts
or
plainer stuff . . .

I don't know

you
young ida
were fourteen years
and already
a dancer

Ballet - "Gipsies"

the jazzer

that's what they call her

she sneaks away from home
into the night
and comes out
to lose herself
at *the palais de danse*

ooh la la

there's all sorts
visit
the palais

and sixteen
and a half years
of age
was never something
to get in the road
of leslie –
squizzy –
taylor

ooh la la

Ballet -"Vive. La France."

*no
detective*

*my leslie
was not afraid
for his life
that morning*

no

*he didn't carry
a gun*

no

*he would never
do that*

no
detective
leslie had no intent
to kill that man

snowy cutmore
was from the fitzroy
push

they were a bad gang
and villains

my leslie
was richmond
through
and through

he would never go . . .

never do . . .

somebody else
must have . .

detective
I do not know

I
cannot tell you

please
leave me
alone now

I would like
to dance

Song and Dance - "My Belgian Rose."

jazz . . .

jazz baby
she used
to be

with her red-gold
hair . . .

well
they called her
beautiful

squizzy
picked her up
when she was just a teen

married
stole and robbed and ran
and hid

squizzy
and *babe*
all over the papers
and
in the courts

then he got shot

murdered –
she knew
nothing
and *just so*
testified –

the coppers
had to let
her go

and watch her
dance
as the years went by

dance
as if
that
was all she'd
ever known

dance
under a new name
that the crowd
bestowed

babe
the jazzer
now
the angel

ida
the favorite
of the fast crowd

ida

angel
of death

Original Sources

1. ida spider (I knew her when): a. Only Melbourne - Mayday Hills Asylum (https://www.onlymelbourne.com.au/mayday-hills-asylum) b. Asylum Ghost Tours, Beechworth (https://www.explorebeechworth.com.au/listing/asylum-ghost-tours-beechworth/)

2. the powerful woman: a. Crime in Carlton: Last Drinks for Squizzy Taylor – 27/10/1927 (http://www.cchg.asn.au/crime.html) b. Partners in Crime: Roberson, Russell, Sydney Morning Herald 03/03/2013 (https://www.smh.com.au/entertainment/tv-and-radio/partners-in-crime-20130302-2fdcv.html)

3. Ida (turning): "Miss Lillias Smith's Pupils Annual Display." The Malvern Standard 03/01/1920 (https://trove.nla.gov.au/newspaper/article/66415131)

4. to be (jazz baby): 'Babe gets her name in the Paper', Croker Prize For Biography Entry 1408. Author unknown (https://dokument.pub/croker-prize-for-biography-entry-1408-babe-gets-her-name-flipbook-pdf.html)

5. the company (she keeps): "Squizzy" Taylor——As He Is! Mirror, Perth 05/07/1924 (https://trove.nla.gov.au/newspaper/article/76437827)

6. dance in the shadows (for leslie): Ida Pender Arrested: The Age (Melbourne) 26/07/1922 (https://trove.nla.gov.au/newspaper/article/205767397)

7. a gun he was (with a drooping eye): "Squizzy's" End: The Sun (Sydney) 28/10/1927 (https://trove.nla.gov.au/newspaper/article/222423476)

8. besotted (said detective piggott): "Ex-Superintendent F. J. Piggott describes" The Herald, Melbourne 06/02/1935 (https://trove.nla.gov.au/newspaper/article/245445312)

9. preserve her purity, yes (but not with us): Batman's Melbourne, The Bulletin, Sydney 10/05/1969 (http://nla.gov.au/nla.obj-1558425715)

10. a shimmer shape (in a scarlet cape): a. Pender Arrested The Age, Melbourne 26/07/1922 (https://trove.nla.gov.au/newspaper/article/205767397) b. The Express and Telegraph, Adelaide 27/07/1922 (https://trove.nla.gov.au/newspaper/article/210611007)

11. as it transpires (I believe) "To See "Squizzy."" Daily Standard, Brisbane 26/09/1924 (http://nla.gov.au/nla.news-article185739673)

12. as important (as an excellent lunch): "St. Kilda Drama" News, Adelaide 13/10/1923 (http://nla.gov.au/nla.news-article129844570)

13. in emergency colours (I'll come back for you): a. "A Prohibited Picture." The Sydney Morning Herald 03/11/1922 (https://trove.nla.gov.au/newspaper/article/16050246) b. Tenille Hands, "Squizzy Taylor, the reel-life gang-star", National Film and Sound Archive. No date provided (https://www.nfsa.gov.au/latest/squizzy-taylor-reel-life-gang-star)

14. meet leslie (we're in the papers): Squizzy Taylor surrenders to police, The Sun, Melbourne 22/09/1922 (https://www.heraldsun.com.au/)

15. I'm ida (who are you): Tenille Hands, "Squizzy Taylor, the reel-life gang-star", National Film and Sound Archive. (https://www.nfsa.gov.au/latest/squizzy-taylor-reel-life-gang-star)

16. there is always the gramophone (I'll show you): "St Kilda Drama" News, Adelaide 13/10/1923 (http://nla.gov.au/nla.news-article129844570)

17. they wear out their tires (then let me go): "Mystery Heroine" The Herald, Melbourne 11/10/1923 (http://nla.gov.au/nla.news-article243736250)

18. tell them nothing (but a lie): ""Squizzy" Taylor Divorced" Truth, Perth 08/03/1924 (http://nla.gov.au/nla.news-article210488201)

19. jobbing dancing (moving): "Ida Pender's Hard Fight To Live Down Unhappy Past" Smith's Weekly, Sydney 09/06/1928 (http://nla.gov.au/nla.news-article234380412)

20. confused (yet right): "Ida Pender's Hard Fight To Live Down Unhappy Past" Smith's Weekly, Sydney 09/06/1928 (https://trove.nla.gov.au/newspaper/article/234380412)

21. long ago (right now): "Ida Pender's Hard Fight To Live Down Unhappy Past" Smith's Weekly, Sydney, 09/06/1928 (https://trove.nla.gov.au/newspaper/article/234380412)

22. ida and squizzy – a summary: Seaside saga, The Age, Melbourne, 2004 (https://www.theage.com.au/national/seaside-saga-20040716-gdy9ob.html)

Author Information

About the Author

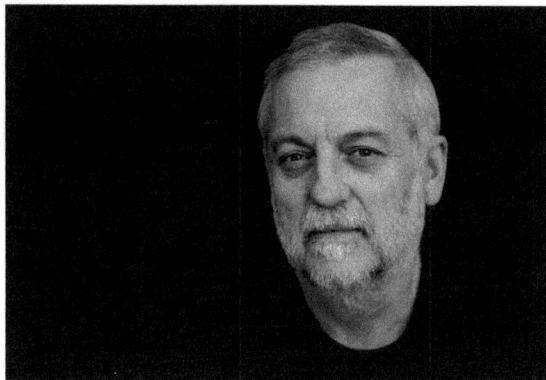

Frank Prem has been a storytelling poet since his teenage years. He has been a psychiatric nurse through all of his professional career, which now exceeds forty years.

He has been published in magazines, online zines, and anthologies in Australia, and in a number of other countries, and has both performed and recorded his work as spoken word.

He lives with his wife in the beautiful township of Beechworth in North East Victoria, Australia.

Connect with Frank

As the author, I hope you enjoyed this volume of poetry collection. I think that mine is a unique style of writing that can appeal well beyond a *'pure poetry'* readership.

If you enjoyed it, I'd like to ask you to do two small things for me.

First, take a moment to find your favourite online retail store and leave a short review of the book in your preferred store.

Online reviews provide social proof to readers and are critical to Indie authors such as myself.

The second thing is, please pop over to my author page **www.FrankPrem. com**, and subscribe to receive my occasional Newsletter.

From time to time I'll let you know what is happening with myself and my writing, as well as keeping you informed of any giveaways I may be planning.

You can also find me on Facebook and Twitter.

Other Published Works

Free Verse Poetry

Small Town Kid (2018)

Devi l In The Wind (2019)
s
The New Asylum (2019)

Herja, Devastation - With Cage Dunn (2019)

Walk Away Silver Heart (2020)

A Kiss for the Worthy (2020)

Rescue and Redemption (2020)

Pebbles to Poems (2020)

The Garden Black (2022)

A Specialist at The Recycled Heart (2022)

Picture Poetry/Spoken Image

Voices (In The Trash) (2020)

The Beechworth Bakery Bears (2021)

Sheep On The Somme (2021)

Waiting For Frank-Bear (2021)

A Lake Sambell Walk (2021)

What Readers Say

Small Town Kid

A modern-day minstrel Small-Town Kid is a wonderful collection —S. T. (Australia)

A poet's walk through his childhood in a small Australian town.—J. L. (USA)

Devil In The Wind

Instantly grips you by the throat in his step-by-step story of survival. Bravo! —K. K. (USA)

Outstanding! —B. T. (Australia)

The New Asylum

Words can't do justice to the emotional journey I travelled. __C. D. (Australia)

If I had to pick one book over the past year that has truly resonated with me, this would be it. __K. B. (USA)

Walk Away Silver Heart

Has an extraordinary way with words. — R C (United States)

As Memorable as My Favorite Music — M D (United States)

A Kiss For The Worthy

A Celebration of Life Written in Thoughtful Bursts of Poetic Expression — M C (United States)

With every verse, I found myself reflecting about myself, my life, and the world —K

Rescue and Redemption

The passion of love in its many forms explored by one for another.—J L (United States)

I've enjoyed every word, every breath. Every moment within the life of these stories.—C D (Australia)

Herja, Devastation

Refreshingly original. Highly recommended! —G. B. (Australia)

Index of Individual Poems

A

a gun he was (with a drooping eye) 28
and so (good night) 75
a shimmer shape (in a scarlet cape) 37
as important (as an excellent lunch) 43
as it transpires (I believe) 39

B

besotted (said detective piggott) 31

C

confused (yet right) 66

D

dance in the shadows (for leslie) 26

I

ida and squizzy - a summary 77
ida spider (I knew her when) 7
ida (turning) 19
I'm ida (who are you) 53
in emergency colours (I'll come back for you) 45

J

jobbing dancing (moving) 63

L

long ago (right now) 69

M

meet leslie (we're in the papers) 49

P

preserve her purity, yes (but not with us) 33

T

tell them nothing (but a lie) 61
the company (she keeps) 25
the powerful woman 13
there is always the gramophone (I'll show you) 56
they wear out their tires (then let me go) 57
to be (jazz baby) 21

www.FrankPrem.com

www.ingramcontent.com/pod-product-compliance
Lightning Source LLC
Chambersburg PA
CBHW070127030426
42335CB00016B/2296